S0-AFV-221

Kansas City, MO Public Library

0000183645415

STEGOSAURUS

Published by The Child's World®
1980 Lookout Drive • Mankato, MN 56003-1705
800-599-READ • www.childsworld.com

Acknowledgments
The Child's World®: Mary Berendes, Publishing Director
The Design Lab: Design
Heidi Schoof: Photo Research
Michael Miller and Sarah Miller: Editing

Content Adviser
Peter Makovicky, PhD, Curator • Field Museum, Chicago, Illinois

Original Cover Art
Todd S. Marshall

Photo Credits
© Albert Copley/Visuals Unlimited, Inc.: 17; Bettmann/Corbis: 7; Charles
George/Visuals Unlimited, Inc.: 13; Corbis: 18; Danny Lehman/Corbis: 26; Dave
G. Houser/Corbis: 24; Francois Gohier/Science Source: 5; Francois Gohier/
Western Paleontological Labs/Science Source: 12; James Marshall/Corbis: 6;
Joe Tucciarone/Science Source: 22, 23; John Shaw/Science Source: 19; Ken
Lucas/Visuals Unlimited, Inc.: 8, 15, 25; Ludek Pesek/Science Source: 9, 21;
Richard Cummins/Corbis: 27; Salisbury District Hospital/Science Source: 11;
slobo/iStockphoto.com: design element (paper); SPL/Science Source: 14

Copyright © 2016 by The Child's World®
All rights reserved. No part of this book may be reproduced or utilized in any
form or by any means without written permission from the publisher.

ISBN 9781631439834
LCCN 2014959661

Printed in the United States of America
Mankato, MN
July, 2015
PA02263

CONTENTS

Spike

It was a warm day, and a gentle rain was falling. The dinosaur had spent most of her morning munching on ferns. But now she stopped eating, walked a little ways, and then lay down. The rain made a soft pattering sound on her thick skin. Today, she just did not feel well. One of her tail spikes had a bad **infection**, and it was not getting any better. The infection had spread throughout her whole body. Now it was making her sick. She closed her heavy eyelids and took one last, deep breath.

Then, 150 million years later, scientists in Colorado found her skeleton. It was embedded in rock. It was broken in places and needed lots of cleaning. And the scientists noticed that one of the tail spikes was different from the others. They were excited to make such a find. The scientists worked on the skeleton for months and months. They decided it belonged to a *Stegosaurus* (steg-oh-SORE-uhss), and it was probably a female. They named her Spike.

This Stegosaurus skeleton at the Royal Tyrrell Museum in Canada is similar to the one discovered by scientists in Colorado. Scientists believe Spike may have become sick from the infection in one of her tail spikes after the spike was somehow broken.

CHAPTER TWO

What Is a Stegosaurus?

A *Stegosaurus* is a dinosaur that lived about 150 million to 144 million years ago. Its name is taken from Greek words that mean "covered lizard" or "roofed lizard." The name refers to the two rows of bony plates that ran along the dinosaur's back. Seventeen triangular plates ran from the dinosaur's neck down

The two pairs of spikes on Stegosaurus's tail were powerful weapons. Unfortunately, although these spikes were often used for protection, they slowed the animal down. Although Stegosaurus could fight with its spiky tail, the dinosaur would have found it difficult to outrun enemies.

to its tail. Around its throat, *Stegosaurus* had a protective bib of bony plates. At the very end of its tail, it had pairs of huge spikes about 3 feet (1 meter) long.

This 1953 visitor to the American Museum of Natural History in New York City compares her foot to the enormous foot of a Stegosaurus skeleton. The front feet of a Stegosaurus each had five toes. Almost like a horse, the tips of these toes were hoof-like. Unlike a horse, however, Stegosaurus was rarely able to move very fast!

Stegosaurus was an enormous **reptile**. It stood about 9 feet (2.75 m) tall. It reached a length of up to 30 feet (9 m). It was about as long and tall as a school bus. Its back legs were twice as long as its front ones. The back legs were long and straight, while the front legs were turned out to the side. Spongy pads covered the bottoms of its short, wide feet.

Despite its huge body, Stegosaurus had a tiny head and brain. Some consider it to be among the least intelligent of the dinosaurs.

Compared with the rest of its body, the animal's head was tiny. In fact, its brain was just a little larger than a golf ball. The dinosaur's mouth ended in a hard beak. The beak helped it tear off parts of plants to eat. It ground the plants with its stubby teeth.

The dinosaur had a large bundle of nerves near the base of its tail. The bundle was so big that scientists once thought it was a second brain. The tail's sharp spikes were great weapons of protection. *Stegosaurus* could **mortally** wound an enemy with one swing of its mighty tail.

The dinosaur reached a weight of 2 to 3 tons (1.8 to 2.7 metric tons) or more. No one knows what color the animal was or whether it had stripes or patterns.

Stegosaurus was hunted by meat-eating predators with amazingly sharp teeth. Fortunately, being hit with Stegosaurus's spiked tail often convinced meat-eating animals to look for their meal somewhere else. Sometimes Stegosaurus successfully scared enemies away by simply swishing its tail from side to side as a warning.

What about Spike's Spike?

Dinosaur bones hold plenty of secrets. They can often tell scientists about how the dinosaur lived and died. By studying bones of living animals, scientists can also learn a lot. They use that knowledge to look at bones of long-dead animals.

For example, after a living animal breaks a bone (like the x-ray of the human bone at right), scar tissue forms around the break. Scar tissue is denser, or thicker, than normal bone tissue. Sometimes scar tissue forms a little bump over the break. When scientists find bones with unusual dense places or bumps, they believe the animal might have had a broken bone that healed. If an animal's bone gets infected, it becomes less dense. In time, it might even be completely eaten away. If the animal cannot fight the infection, it could spread throughout its whole body.

One of Spike's tail spikes looked badly infected when she died. The spike was flatter and shorter than it should have been. With that painful spike, maybe the dinosaur had a hard time defending herself. Maybe she just kept feeling worse and worse all the time. We will never know exactly why Spike died, but her bones tell us some of her story.

CHAPTER THREE

Who Found the First Stegosaurus?

In 1876, M. P. Felch discovered the bones of a *Stegosaurus* in Colorado. The following year, his boss, Othniel Charles Marsh, described it to the scientific world. Marsh was a famous paleontologist (pay-lee-un-TAWL-uh-jist) at the time. Paleontologists study fossils. Fossils are the remains

Felch found Stegosaurus bones in Colorado, but Stegosaurus lived in other parts of North America, too. Additional fossils have been found in Wyoming and Utah.

of **ancient** life, such as bones and imprints of leaves.

Sometimes paleontologists find only a few bones of an animal. Then they have a tough job of figuring out what kind of animal it was. Sometimes they find a dinosaur skeleton that is broken and scattered everywhere. Then they have to figure out how it all fits together. Sometimes they find dinosaur eggs and sometimes only footprints. Still, each of these fossils tells them something about a dinosaur and how it lived.

A fossil of an Oviraptor still inside its egg. Oviraptors lived in a different time than Stegosaurus did and were much smaller and faster.

Othniel Charles Marsh named several species of dinosaur besides Stegosaurus. A few of the more famous dinosaurs he named were Triceratops, Allosaurus, Diplodocus, and Apatosaurus.

By looking at the *Stegosaurus* fossils, Marsh first thought that the animal's plates laid down flat on its back. But over the next ten years, Marsh and his workers made more exciting discoveries. One of the best finds was a *Stegosaurus* skeleton with the bones and plates laid out almost perfectly. Now it was clear that those plates stood up along the dinosaur's back. Still, everyone wondered what they were for.

CHAPTER FOUR

Why Did It Have Those Plates?

Some scientists believed that the plates might have been for protection. But others pointed out that the plates would not have been much help. After all, an attacking dinosaur could just bite

Scientists believe that Stegosaurus may have been able to move the hard plates on its back to attract a mate or frighten an enemy. Moving special muscles under the skin may have allowed the dinosaur to flap the plates back and forth.

Stegosaurus in the side. Some scientists today believe that the plates were used for **display**. Maybe the male showed off his plates to attract a female. Maybe the dinosaur stiffened its back and showed those plates to scare off enemies.

Other scientists believe that the plates helped the dinosaur in another way. They have looked closely and found that the plates were not solid. They had tiny tunnels running through them. These tunnels might have been for blood vessels. If *Stegosaurus* needed to warm up, it could have stood in the sun. The blood running through the plates would have warmed up the animal quickly. If *Stegosaurus* was too hot, breezes passing by the plates might have cooled down the animal.

If Stegosaurus used the plates on its back to control body temperature, many scientists believe that the dinosaur may have been cold blooded. This means that Stegosaurus's body temperature would have depended on the outside temperature.

How Did Stegosaurus Spend Its Time?

This drawing shows a Stegosaurus eating low-lying plants. Although many scientists believe that Stegosaurus always remained on all fours, some think it may have reared up on its back legs to reach food higher up. While it might be hard to imagine an animal as large and bulky as Stegosaurus doing this, scientists point out that this is how many elephants get their food.

To feed its huge body, *Stegosaurus* probably spent most of its day eating. *Stegosaurus* was an herbivore (UR-buh-vore). This means that it ate only plants. Its head was low to the ground, so it probably could not reach food more than 3 feet (1 m) high. Some paleontologists believe that *Stegosaurus* was able to stand up on its back legs. By doing this, it could reach higher food. But because no one can watch a live *Stegosaurus* as it eats, we may never know.

The plant life in Olympic National Forest in Washington is similar to what Stegosaurus would have eaten while it lived. Moss and ferns were soft plants that would have been easy for Stegosaurus to eat, given the dinosaur's stubby, weak teeth.

Stegosaurus did not eat grass because grass had not yet appeared on Earth. Instead, it probably ate ferns and plants called **horsetails**, club mosses, and **conifers**. These grew easily in the warm, humid **environment** of the Jurassic (ju-RASS-ik) period.

CHAPTER SIX

What Was the Jurassic Period?

The Jurassic period was the time span from about 208 million years ago to about 144 million years ago. During that time, Earth was very different from how it is today. Scientists believe that most of Earth's large landmasses (now known as continents) were packed very closely together. During the 64 million years of the Jurassic period, they slowly drifted apart.

Earth was also much warmer than it is now. At the North and South Poles, the air was cool, but not cold. The poles were not even covered with ice. The sea level was higher all over Earth. Many places were lush and green. There was plenty of food for giant, plant-eating dinosaurs.

An artist's idea of what the landscape might have looked like during the Jurassic period. Dinosaurs mysteriously disappeared from Earth during the following period, the Cretaceous (kreh-TAY-shuss) period.

Dinosaurs dominated Earth during this time. *Stegosaurus* walked the lands now known as North America, Africa, Europe, and Asia. Other giant plant-eaters, such as *Diplodocus* (dih-PLOD-uh-kuss) and *Apatosaurus* (uh-pat-oh-SORE-uhss), also roamed about. Sharks and huge saltwater crocodiles swam in

Brachiosaurus was a giant plant-eater that existed during the Jurassic period. For a while, scientists incorrectly believed that, like Stegosaurus, Brachiosaurus had a second brain.

the oceans. Flying reptiles and the first birds circled overhead. Some of the first mammals, tiny mouse-sized creatures, rustled about on the ground.

Spinosaurus was one of the dinosaurs that existed during the Cretaceous period. This dinosaur had a series of spines that formed what looked like a fin on its back. Like the plates on Stegosaurus's back, these spines may have been used to attract mates, frighten enemies, or help control body temperature.

Stegosaurus died out around 144 million years ago, just as the Jurassic period was coming to an end. About 77 million years later, the great *Tyrannosaurus rex* appeared. About 65 million years after that, human beings first walked Earth.

Have you ever seen a dinosaur skeleton in a museum? Did you ever wonder how scientists knew which bones went where? When scientists discover a dinosaur skeleton, they take a long look at how the bones are laid out. Sometimes the skeleton is a big mess, with broken bones spread everywhere. But once in a while, a skeleton seems to be laid out nicely.

Paleontologists always take lots of notes and pictures when they find a good skeleton because this helps them put it together later. And every time they find a new skeleton, they learn more about the dinosaur.

Stegosaurus plates
puzzled everyone for a long
time. First, Marsh thought
they laid down flat. Later,
paleontologists thought
they pointed straight up and
formed a single row down the
dinosaur's back. Museums
around the world set up their
Stegosaurus skeletons to

match this idea. In time, more skeletons were discovered.
Scientists learned more about the creatures with each
new find. Now they think the plates were in two rows,
with one plate leaning to the left and the next plate
leaning to the right. Today, workers at some museums are
taking off the plates of their old *Stegosaurus* skeletons.
They are rebuilding the skeletons to fit this new idea.

What Else Can We Learn?

Everything we know about *Stegosaurus* and other dinosaurs comes from the fossils they left behind. Sometimes paleontologists find fossils of plant materials where the dinosaur's stomach would have been. This gives them clues as to what the dinosaur probably ate. Sometimes imprints from ancient plants are found near the

In addition to showing how fast a dinosaur moved, footprints can also tell scientists where certain dinosaurs lived and whether they traveled alone or in herds.

These dinosaur skeletons are at the Museum of Natural History in Houston, Texas. Museums sometimes exhibit the original skeletons, but sometimes they show casts, or copies, instead. Dinosaur bones are rare and delicate and are often stored in special museum collections where they are less likely to be damaged.

dinosaur. These tell scientists what kinds of plants were in the animal's environment. Sometimes dinosaur footprints give clues as to how fast the animal moved. Still, there are many questions about *Stegosaurus* that no one has answered. Could it really stand up on its hind legs? How much did it eat every day? How fast could it run? And why did it die out? Paleontologists have puzzled over these questions for years. Maybe someday, you will help solve some of these mysteries.

GLOSSARY

ancient (AYN-shunt) Something that is ancient is very old—from millions of years ago. Fossils are remains of ancient life.

conifers (KON-uh-furz) Conifers are plants that have cones. *Stegosaurus* probably ate conifers.

display (diss-PLAY) A display is a show, or the act of showing off. The plates on *Stegosaurus* may have been used for display.

environment (en-VYE-ruhn-muhnt) An environment is made up of the things that surround a living creature, such as the air and soil. Scientists can sometimes tell what kind of plants were in an ancient animal's environment by studying fossils.

horsetails (HORSS-taylz) Horsetails are ancient stick-like plants. *Stegosaurus* probably ate horsetails.

infection (in-FEK-shuhn) An infection is a disease caused by germs. It was possible for *Stegosaurus* to develop an infection in one of its spikes.

mortally (MOR-tuhl-lee) Mortally describes an action causing death. *Stegosaurus* could use its spiky tail to mortally wound an enemy.

reptile (REP-tile) A reptile is an air-breathing animal with a backbone and is usually covered with scales or plates. *Stegosaurus* was a reptile.

TRIASSIC PERIOD

Date: 248 million to 208 million years ago
Fossils: *Coelophysis, Cynodont, Desmatosuchus, Eoraptor, Gerrothorax, Peteinoaurus, Placerias, Plateosaurus, Postosuchus, Procompsognathus, Riojasaurus, Saltopus, Teratosaurus, Thecodontosaurus*

Distinguishing Features: For the most part, the climate in the Triassic period was hot and dry. The first true mammals appeared during this period, as well as turtles, frogs, salamanders, and lizards. Corals could also be found in oceans at this time, although large reefs such as the ones we have today did not yet exist. Evergreen trees made up much of the plant life.

JURASSIC PERIOD

Date: 208 million to 144 million years ago
Fossils: *Allosaurus, Apatosaurus, Brachiosaurus, Compsognathus, Dilophosaurus, Diplodocus, Hybodus, Kentrosaurus, Megalosaurus, Saurolophus, Segisaurus, Seismosaurus, Stegosaurus, Supersaurus, Ultrasaurus, Vulcanodon*

Distinguishing Features: The climate of the Jurassic period was warm and moist. The first birds appeared during this period. Plant life was also greener and more widespread. Sharks began swimming in Earth's oceans. Although dinosaurs did not even exist at the beginning of the Triassic period, they ruled Earth by Jurassic times. A minor mass extinction occurred toward the end of the Jurassic period.

THE GEOLOGIC TIME SCALE

CRETACEOUS PERIOD

Date: 144 million to 65 million years ago
Fossils: *Alamosaurus, Albertosaurus, Ankylosaurus, Argentinosaurus, Bagaceratops, Baryonyx, Carnotaurus, Centrosaurus, Corythosaurus, Didelphodon, Edmontonia, Edmontosaurus, Gallimimus, Gigantosaurus, Hadrosaurus, Hypsilophodon, Iguanodon, Kronosaurus, Lambeosaurus, Maiasaura, Megaraptor, Nodosaurus, Oviraptor, Parasaurolophus, Protoceratops, Psittacosaurus, Saltasaurus, Sarcosuchus, Saurolophus, Sauropelta, Saurornithoides, Segnosaurus, Spinosaurus, Stygimoloch, Styracosaurus, Tarbosaurus, Thescelosaurus, Torosaurus, Trachodon, Triceratops, Troodon, Tyrannosaurus rex, Utahraptor, Velociraptor*

Distinguishing Features: The climate of the Cretaceous period was fairly mild. Flowering plants first appeared in this period, and many modern plants developed. With flowering plants came a greater diversity of insect life. Birds further developed into two types: flying and flightless. A wider variety of mammals also existed. At the end of this period came a great mass extinction that wiped out the dinosaurs, along with several other groups of animals.

DID YOU KNOW?

- *Stegosaurus* is the state fossil of Colorado.

- It took a U.S. Army helicopter to carry Spike's skeleton to a place where scientists could work on it.

- Some *Stegosaurus* had large spines sticking out from their shoulders.

- A *Stegosaurus* skeleton discovered by M. P. Felch is now on display in a museum where people have nicknamed it 'The Roadkill.'

HOW TO LEARN MORE

At the Library

Lambert, David, Darren Naish, and Liz Wyse. *Dinosaur Encyclopedia*. New York, NY: DK Publishing, 2001.

Landau, Elaine. *Stegosaurus*. New York, NY: Children's Press, 2007.

On the Web

Visit our Web site for links about *Stegosaurus*: **childsworld.com/links**

Note to Parents, Teachers, and Librarians: We routinely verify our Web links to make sure they are safe and active sites. So encourage your readers to check them out!

Places to Visit or Contact

American Museum of Natural History: *To view numerous dinosaur fossils, as well as the fossils of several ancient mammals*
Address: Central Park West at 79th Street, New York, NY 10024
Phone: (212) 769-5100

Carnegie Museum of Natural History: *To view a variety of dinosaur skeletons, as well as fossils related to other reptiles, amphibians, and fish that are now extinct*
Address: 4400 Forbes Avenue, Pittsburgh, PA 15213
Phone: (412) 622-3131

Dinosaur Depot: *To see the dinosaur named Spike*
Address: 330 Royal Gorge Blvd., Cañon City, CO 81212
Phone: (800) 987-6379

Dinosaur National Monument: *To view a huge deposit of dinosaur bones in a natural setting*
Address: 4545 East Highway 40, Dinosaur, CO 81610
Phone: (970) 374-3000
 −OR−
Dinosaur National Monument (Quarry):
Address: 11625 East 1500 South, Jensen, UT 84035
Phone: (435) 781-7700

Museum of the Rockies: *To see real dinosaur fossils, as well as robotic replicas*
Address: Montana State University, 600 West Kagy Boulevard, Bozeman, MT 59717
Phone: (406) 994-2251 or (406) 994-DINO

National Museum of Natural History (Smithsonian Institution): *To see several dinosaur exhibits and take special behind-the-scenes tours*
Address: 10th Street and Constitution Avenue, N.W., Washington, DC 20560
Phone: (202) 357-2700

INDEX

ABOUT THE AUTHOR

Susan H. Gray has bachelor's and master's degrees in zoology and has taught college-level courses in biology. She first fell in love with fossil hunting while studying paleontology in college. In her 25 years as an author, she has written many articles for scientists and researchers, and many science books for children. Susan enjoys gardening, traveling, and playing the piano. She and her husband, Michael, live in Cabot, Arkansas.